FUZZY PINK

EASY

Shown on page 1.

Finished Size: One size fits most women

MATERIALS

Bulky Weight Yarn (BULKY 5)
[$1^3/_4$ ounces, 71 yards
(50 grams, 65 meters) per skein]:
20 skeins
Crochet hook, size K (6.5 mm) **or** size needed for gauge
Safety pin
Yarn needle

GAUGE: In pattern,
13 sts = 4" (10 cm);
8 rows = $4^1/_4$" (10.75 cm)

Gauge Swatch: 4"w x $4^1/_4$"
(10 cm x 10.75 cm)
Ch 15.
Work same as Front for 8 rows.
Finish off.

FRONT

Ch 129.

Row 1 (Right side)**:** Dc in fourth ch from hook **(3 skipped chs count as first dc)** and in each ch across: 127 dc.

Note: Loop a short piece of yarn around any stitch to mark Row 1 as **right** side.

Row 2: Ch 5 **(counts as first dc plus ch 2, now and throughout)**, turn; skip next 2 dc, dc in next dc, ★ ch 2, skip next 2 dc, dc in next dc; repeat from ★ across: 43 dc and 42 ch-2 sps.

Row 3: Ch 3 **(counts as first dc, now and throughout)**, turn; (2 dc in next ch-2 sp, dc in next dc) across: 127 dc.

Repeat Rows 2 and 3 for pattern until piece measures approximately 24" (61 cm) from beginning ch, ending by working Row 3.

NECK SHAPING

RIGHT SIDE

Row 1 (Wrong side)**:** Ch 5, turn; skip next 2 dc, dc in next dc, ★ ch 2, skip next 2 dc, dc in next dc; repeat from ★ 13 times **more**, leave remaining 81 dc unworked: 16 dc and 15 ch-2 sps.

Row 2: Ch 3, turn; (2 dc in next ch-2 sp, dc in next dc) across; place loop from hook on safety pin to keep piece from unraveling as you work Left Side: 46 dc.

LEFT SIDE

Row 1: With **wrong** side facing, skip next 35 dc from Right Side and join yarn with slip st in next dc; ch 5, skip next 2 dc, dc in next dc, ★ ch 2, skip next 2 dc, dc in next dc; repeat from ★ across: 16 dc and 15 ch-2 sps.

Row 2: Ch 3, turn; (2 dc in next ch-2 sp, dc in next dc) across; finish off: 46 dc.

BACK

Row 1: With **wrong** side facing, remove safety pin and place loop onto hook; ch 5, skip next 2 dc, dc in next dc, ★ ch 2, skip next 2 dc, dc in next dc; repeat from ★ across Right Side; ch 35 for back neck edge; working across dc of Left Side, dc in first dc, ★ ch 2, skip next 2 dc, dc in next dc; repeat from ★ across: 32 dc and 30 ch-2 sps.

Row 2: Ch 3, turn; (2 dc in next ch-2 sp, dc in next dc) 15 times, dc in next 35 chs and in next dc, (2 dc in next ch-2 sp, dc in next dc) across: 127 dc.

Row 3: Ch 5, turn; skip next 2 dc, dc in next dc, ★ ch 2, skip next 2 dc, dc in next dc; repeat from ★ across: 43 dc and 42 ch-2 sps.

Row 4: Ch 3, turn; (2 dc in next ch-2 sp, dc in next dc) across: 127 dc.

Repeat Rows 3 and 4 for pattern until Back measures approximately 24" (61 cm) from back neck edge, ending by working Row 4.

Finish off.

TASSEL (Make 4)

Cut a piece of cardboard 3" (7.5 cm) wide and 8" (20.5 cm) long. Wind a double strand of yarn around the cardboard approximately 25 times. Cut an 18" (40.5 cm) length of yarn and insert it under all of the strands at the top of the cardboard; pull up **tightly** and tie securely. Leave the yarn ends long enough to attach the tassel. Cut the yarn at the opposite end of the cardboard and then remove it ***(Fig. 1a)***. Cut an 8" (20.5 cm) length of yarn and wrap it **tightly** around the tassel twice, $1^1/_2$" (4 cm) below the top ***(Fig. 1b)***; tie securely. Trim the ends.
Sew one tassel to each corner of Poncho.

Fig. 1a

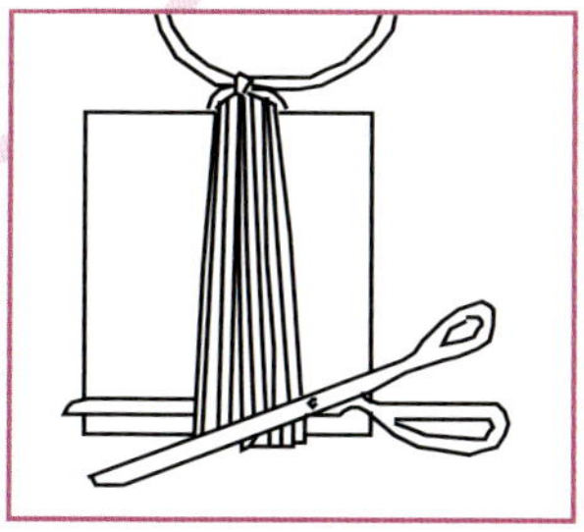

Fig. 1b

STRIPES

EASY

Shown on page 5.

Finished Size	**Misses Size** (approximate)
Small	4-6
Medium	8-10
Large	12-14
X-Large	16-18

Size Note: Instructions are written for size Small with sizes Medium, Large, and X-Large in braces { }. Instructions will be easier to read if you circle all the numbers pertaining to your size. If only one number is given, it applies to all sizes.

MATERIALS

Light/Worsted Weight Yarn (LIGHT 3)
[$3^1/_2$ ounces, 250 yards (100 grams, 230 meters) per skein]:
Orange, Red, and Green - 1{2-2-3} skeins **each** color
Crochet hook, size H (5 mm) **or** size needed for gauge

GAUGE: In pattern,
15 dc and 9 rows = 4" (10 cm)

Gauge Swatch: 4" (10 cm) square
Ch 12.
Row 1: Dc in fourth ch from hook **(3 skipped chs count as first dc)** and in each ch across: 10 dc.
Rows 2-9: Ch 3 **(counts as first dc)**, turn; dc in next dc and in each dc across.
Finish off.

Instructions begin on page 4.

Stripe Sequence: One round each: ★ Orange, Red, Green; repeat from ★ for Stripe Sequence.

Note: Poncho is made in one piece circularly from the top down.

PONCHO

With Orange, ch 84; being careful not to twist ch, join with slip st to form a ring.

Eyelet Rnd: Ch 4 (**counts as first dc plus ch 1**), skip next ch, ★ dc in next ch, ch 1, skip next ch; repeat from ★ around; join with slip st to first dc changing to Red ***(Fig. 2)***: 42 dc and 42 ch-1 sps.

Fig. 2

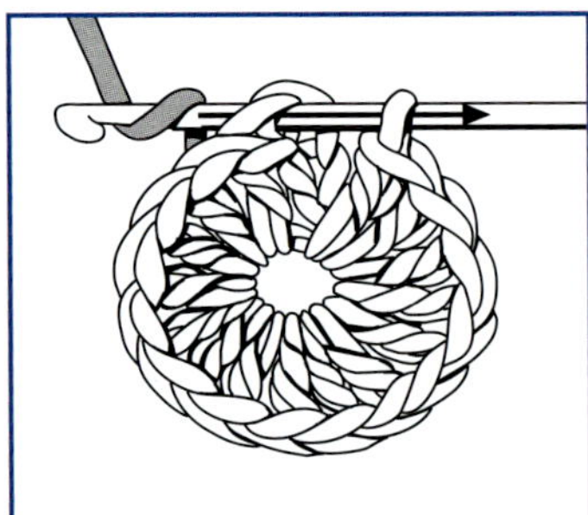

Rnd 1 (Right side)**:** Ch 3 (**counts as first dc, now and throughout**), dc in next ch-1 sp, (dc in next dc and in next ch-1 sp) 4 times, (dc, ch 1, dc) in next dc, (dc in next ch-1 sp and in next dc) 10 times, (dc, ch 1, dc) in next ch-1 sp, (dc in next dc and in next ch-1 sp) 10 times, (dc, ch 1, dc) in next dc, (dc in next ch-1 sp and in next dc) 10 times, (dc, ch 1, dc) in next ch-1 sp, (dc in next dc and in next ch-1 sp) 5 times; join with slip st to first dc changing to Green: 22 dc between each corner ch-1 sp.

Rnd 2: Ch 3, dc in next dc and in each dc around working (dc, ch 1, dc) in each corner ch-1 sp; join with slip st to first dc changing to Orange: 24 dc between each corner ch-1 sp.

Maintaining Stripe Sequence, repeat Rnd 2 until there are 40{44-48-52} dc between each corner ch-1 sp.

Next Rnd: Ch 3, ★ dc in next dc and in each dc across to next ch-1 sp, (dc, ch 1, dc) in ch-1 sp, dc in next dc and in each dc across to next ch-1 sp, 2 dc in ch-1 sp; repeat from ★ once **more**, dc in next dc and in each dc to across; join with slip st to first dc changing to next color: 168{184-200-216} dc and 2 ch-1 sps.

Next Rnd: Ch 3, ★ dc in next dc and in each dc across to next ch-1 sp, (dc, ch 1, dc) in ch-1 sp; repeat from ★ once **more**, dc in next dc and in each dc across; join with slip st to first dc changing to next color: 172{188-204-220} dc and 2 ch-1 sps.

Maintaining Stripe Sequence, repeat last round until Poncho measures approximately 16" (40.5 cm) from beginning ch **or** to desired length.

Finish off.

TIE

With Red, ch 240.

Slip st in back ridge of second ch from hook ***(Fig. 5a, page 12)*** and each ch across; finish off.

Beginning at center front, weave tie through ch-1 sps on Eyelet Rnd; tie in a bow.

SASSY SALSA

EASY

Finished Size: One size fits most women

MATERIALS

Bulky Weight Yarn (BULKY 5)
[1³/₄ ounces, 76 yards
(50 grams, 70 meters) per skein]:
10 skeins
Crochet hook, size K (6.5 mm) **or** size needed for gauge
Yarn needle

GAUGE: In pattern,
13 sts and 12 rows = 4" (10 cm)

Gauge Swatch: 4" (10 cm) square
Ch 14.
Work same as Rectangle for 12 rows.
Finish off.

RECTANGLE (Make 2)

Ch 80.

Row 1 (Right side)**:** Sc in second ch from hook, ★ ch 1, skip next ch, sc in next ch; repeat from ★ across: 40 sc and 39 ch-1 sps.

Note: Loop a short piece of yarn around any stitch to mark Row 1 as **right** side.

Row 2: Ch 1, turn; sc in first sc and in next ch-1 sp, ch 1, (sc in next ch-1 sp, ch 1) across to last ch-1 sp, sc in last ch-1 sp and in last sc: 41 sc and 38 ch-1 sps.

Row 3: Ch 1, turn; sc in first sc, ch 1, (sc in next ch-1 sp, ch 1) across to last 2 sc, skip next sc, sc in last sc: 40 sc and 39 ch-1 sps.

Repeat Rows 2 and 3 until piece measures approximately 16" (40.5 cm) from beginning ch, ending by working Row 3.

Finish off.

FINISHING

With **right** sides facing and using diagram as a guide, sew rectangles together.

Diagram

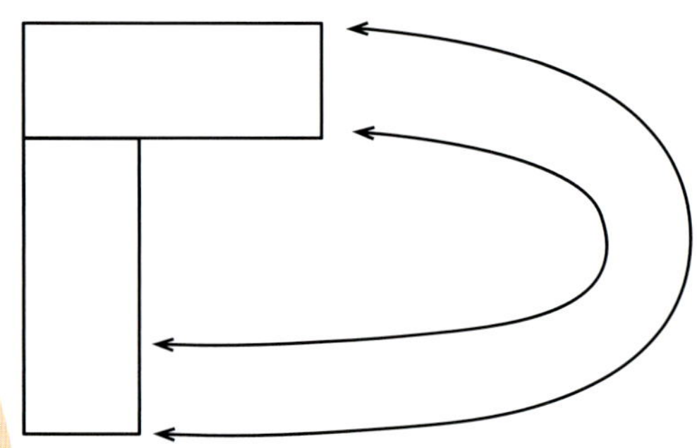

FRINGE

Add fringe evenly around lower edges as follows: Cut a piece of cardboard 5" (12.5 cm) wide and 9" (23 cm) long. Wind the yarn **loosely** and **evenly** lengthwise around the cardboard until the card is filled, then cut across one end; repeat as needed. Hold together 3 strands of yarn; fold in half.
With **wrong** side facing and using a crochet hook, draw the folded end up through a stitch or space and pull the loose ends through the folded end ***(Fig. 3a)***; draw the knot up **tightly** ***(Fig. 3b)***.
Repeat, spacing as desired.
Lay flat on a hard surface and trim the ends.

Fig. 3a

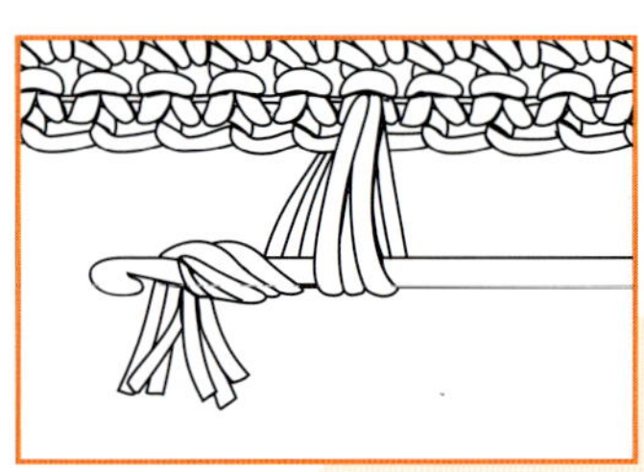

Fig. 3b

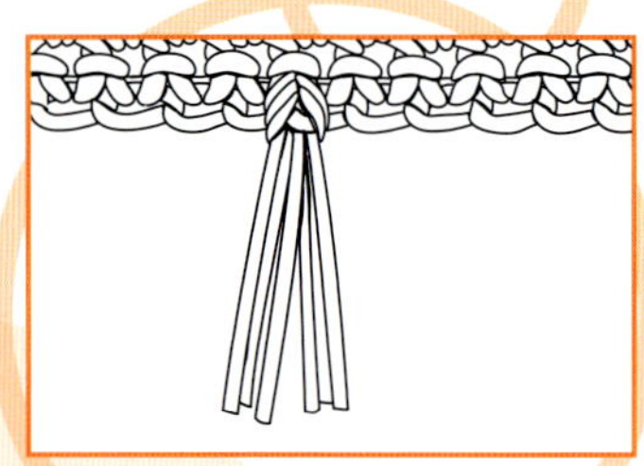

CIRCULAR JADE

EASY

Finished Size: One size fits most women

MATERIALS

MEDIUM 4

Medium/Worsted Weight Yarn
[5 ounces, 253 yards
(140 grams, 231 meters) per skein]:
2 skeins
Crochet hook, size I (5.5 mm) **or** size needed for gauge
3/8" (10 mm) Ribbon - 48" (122 cm) length

GAUGE: In pattern,
14 dc and 8 rnds = 4" (10 cm)

Gauge Swatch: 4" (10 cm) square
Ch 16.
Row 1: Dc in fourth ch from hook **(3 skipped chs count as first dc)** and in each ch across: 14 dc.
Rows 2-8: Ch 3 **(counts as first dc)**, turn; dc in next dc and in each dc across.
Finish off.

Note: Poncho is made in one piece circularly from the top down.

PONCHO

Ch 77; being careful not to twist ch, join with slip st to form a ring.

Rnd 1 (Right side)**:** Ch 3 **(counts as first dc, now and throughout)**, dc in next ch and in each ch around; join with slip st to first dc: 77 dc.

Rnd 2: Ch 3, dc in same st and in next 6 dc, (2 dc in next dc, dc in next 6 dc) around; join with slip st to first dc: 88 dc.

Rnd 3 (Eyelet rnd)**:** Ch 3, dc in next dc, ch 2, skip next 2 dc, ★ dc in next 2 dc, ch 2, skip next 2 dc; repeat from ★ around; join with slip st to first dc: 44 dc and 22 ch-2 sps.

Rnd 4: Ch 3, dc in next dc, 2 dc in next ch-2 sp, dc in next 2 dc, 3 dc in next ch-2 sp, ★ dc in next 2 dc, 2 dc in next ch-2 sp, dc in next 2 dc, 3 dc in next ch-2 sp; repeat from ★ around; join with slip st to first dc: 99 dc.

Rnd 5: Ch 3, dc in next dc and in each dc around; join with slip st to first dc.

Rnd 6: Ch 3, dc in same st and in next 8 dc, (2 dc in next dc, dc in next 8 dc) around; join with slip st to first dc: 110 dc.

Rnd 7: Ch 3, dc in next dc and in each dc around; join with slip st to first dc.

Rnd 8: Ch 3, dc in same st and in next 9 dc, (2 dc in next dc, dc in next 9 dc) around; join with slip st to first dc: 121 dc.

Rnd 9: Ch 3, dc in next dc and in each dc around; join with slip st to first dc.

Rnd 10: Ch 3, dc in same st and in next 10 dc, (2 dc in next dc, dc in next 10 dc) around; join with slip st to first dc: 132 dc.

Rnd 11: Ch 3, dc in next dc, ch 2, skip next 2 dc, ★ dc in next 2 dc, ch 2, skip next 2 dc; repeat from ★ around; join with slip st to first dc: 66 dc and 33 ch-2 sps.

Rnd 12: Ch 3, dc in next dc, (2 dc in next ch-2 sp, dc in next 2 dc) twice, 3 dc in next ch-2 sp, ★ dc in next 2 dc, (2 dc in next ch-2 sp, dc in next 2 dc) twice, 3 dc in next ch-2 sp; repeat from ★ around; join with slip st to first dc: 143 dc.

Rnd 13: Ch 3, dc in next dc and in each dc around; join with slip st to first dc.

Rnd 14: Ch 3, dc in same st and in next 12 dc, (2 dc in next dc, dc in next 12 dc) around; join with slip st to first dc: 154 dc.

Instructions continued on page 10.

Rnd 15: Ch 3, dc in next dc and in each dc around; join with slip st to first dc.

Rnd 16: Ch 3, dc in same st and in next 13 dc, (2 dc in next dc, dc in next 13 dc) around; join with slip st to first dc: 165 dc.

Rnd 17: Ch 3, dc in next dc and in each dc around; join with slip st to first dc.

Rnd 18: Ch 3, dc in same st and in next 14 dc, (2 dc in next dc, dc in next 14 dc) around; join with slip st to first dc: 176 dc.

Rnd 19: Ch 3, dc in next dc, ch 2, skip next 2 dc, ★ dc in next 2 dc, ch 2, skip next 2 dc; repeat from ★ around; join with slip st to first dc: 88 dc and 44 ch-2 sps.

Rnd 20: Ch 3, dc in next dc, (2 dc in next ch-2 sp, dc in next 2 dc) 3 times, 3 dc in next ch-2 sp, ★ dc in next 2 dc, (2 dc in next ch-2 sp, dc in next 2 dc) 3 times, 3 dc in next ch-2 sp; repeat from ★ around; join with slip st to first dc: 187 dc.

Rnd 21: Ch 3, dc in same st and in each dc around; join with slip st to first dc: 188 dc.

Rnds 22-26: Ch 3, dc in next dc and in each dc around; join with slip st to first dc.

Rnd 27: Ch 3, dc in next dc, ch 2, skip next 2 dc, ★ dc in next 2 dc, ch 2, skip next 2 dc; repeat from ★ around; join with slip st to first dc: 94 dc and 47 ch-2 sps.

Rnd 28: Slip st in next dc and in next ch-2 sp, ch 1, (sc, 3 dc, sc) in same sp and in each ch-2 sp around; join with slip st to first sc, finish off.

Using photo as a guide, weave ribbon through ch-2 sps on Eyelet Rnd; tie in a bow.

YARN INFORMATION

Each Poncho in this leaflet was made with Light/Worsted, Medium/Worsted, or Bulky Weight Yarn. Any brand of Light/Worsted, Medium/Worsted, or Bulky Weight Yarn may be used. It is best to refer to the yardage/meters when determining how many balls or skeins to purchase. Remember, to arrive at the finished size, it is the GAUGE/TENSION that is important, not the brand of yarn.

For your convenience, listed below are the specific yarns used to create our photography models.

FUZZY PINK
Moda Dea™ Aerie™
#9788 Pink

STRIPES
TLC® Wiggles™
Orange = #209 Orange
Red = #322 Red
Green = #727 Green

SASSY SALSA
Moda Dea™ Ricochet™
#2942 Mambo

CIRCULAR JADE
TLC® Lustre™
#5507 Bright Jade

GENERAL INSTRUCTIONS

ABBREVIATIONS

ch(s)	chain(s)
cm	centimeters
dc	double crochet(s)
mm	millimeters
Rnd(s)	Round(s)
sc	single crochet(s)
sp(s)	space(s)
st(s)	stitch(es)

★ — work instructions following ★ as many **more** times as indicated in addition to the first time.

( ) or [ ] — work enclosed instructions **as many** times as specified by the number immediately following **or** work all enclosed instructions in the stitch or space indicated **or** contains explanatory remarks.

colon (:) — the number(s) given after a colon at the end of a row or round denote(s) the number of stitches or spaces you should have on that row or round.

CROCHET TERMINOLOGY		
UNITED STATES		**INTERNATIONAL**
slip stitch (slip st)	=	single crochet (sc)
single crochet (sc)	=	double crochet (dc)
half double crochet (hdc)	=	half treble crochet (htr)
double crochet (dc)	=	treble crochet (tr)
treble crochet (tr)	=	double treble crochet (dtr)
double treble crochet (dtr)	=	triple treble crochet (ttr)
triple treble crochet (tr tr)	=	quadruple treble crochet (qtr)
skip	=	miss

GAUGE

Exact gauge is **essential** for proper fit. Before beginning your Poncho, make the sample swatch given in the individual instructions in the yarn and hook specified. After completing the swatch, measure it, counting your stitches and rows or rounds carefully. If your swatch is larger or smaller than specified, **make another, changing hook size to get the correct gauge**. Keep trying until you find the size hook that will give you the specified gauge.

HINTS

As in all crocheted pieces, good finishing techniques make a big difference in the quality of the piece. Make a habit of taking care of loose ends as you work. Thread a yarn needle with the yarn end. With **wrong** side facing, weave the needle through several stitches, then reverse the direction and weave it back through several stitches. When ends are secure, clip them off close to work.

Yarn Weight Symbol & Names	SUPER FINE 1	FINE 2	LIGHT 3	MEDIUM 4	BULKY 5	SUPER BULKY 6
Type of Yarns in Category	Sock, Fingering Baby	Sport, Baby	DK, Light Worsted	Worsted, Afghan, Aran	Chunky, Craft, Rug	Bulky, Roving

ALUMINUM CROCHET HOOKS													
U.S.	B-1	C-2	D-3	E-4	F-5	G-6	H-8	I-9	J-10	K-10½	N	P	Q
Metric - mm	2.25	2.75	3.25	3.5	3.75	4	5	5.5	6	6.5	9	10	15

BEGINNER	Projects for first-time crocheters using basic stitches. Minimal shaping.
EASY	Projects using yarn with basic stitches, repetitive stitch patterns, simple color changes, and simple shaping and finishing.
INTERMEDIATE	Projects using a variety of techniques, such as basic lace patterns or color patterns, mid-level shaping and finishing.
EXPERIENCED	Projects with intricate stitch patterns, techniques and dimension, such as non-repeating patterns, multi-color techniques, fine threads, small hooks, detailed shaping and refined finishing.

BASIC STITCHES

CHAIN

To work a chain stitch, begin with a slip knot on the hook. Bring the yarn **over** hook from back to front, catching the yarn with the hook and turning the hook slightly toward you to keep the yarn from slipping off. Draw the yarn through the slip knot ***(Fig. 4)*** **(first chain st made, *abbreviated ch*)**.

Fig. 4

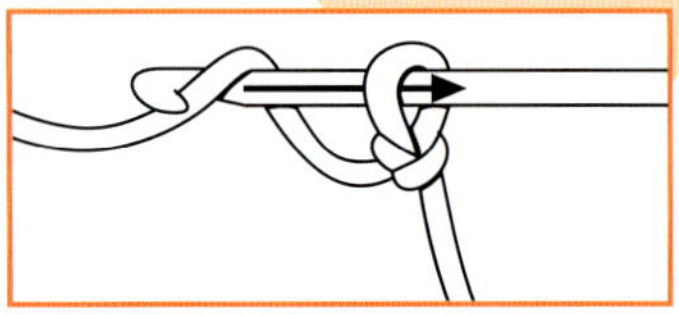

WORKING INTO THE CHAIN

Method 1: Insert hook into back ridge of each chain ***(Fig. 5a)***.

Method 2: Insert hook under top two strands of each chain ***(Fig. 5b)***.

Method 3: To form a ring, work the specified number of chains and then join to the first chain made with a slip st ***(Fig. 5c)***.

Fig. 5a

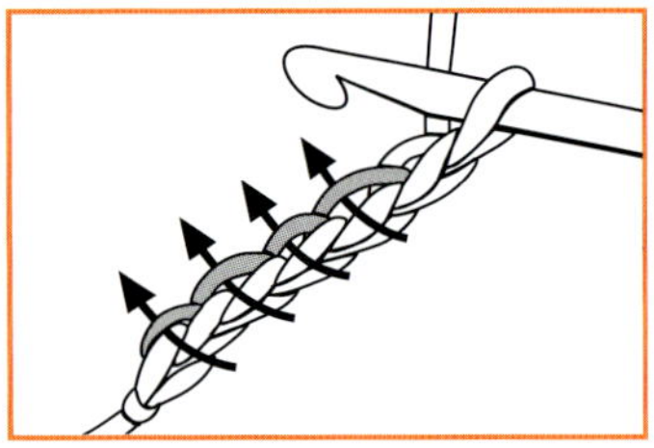

Fig. 5b

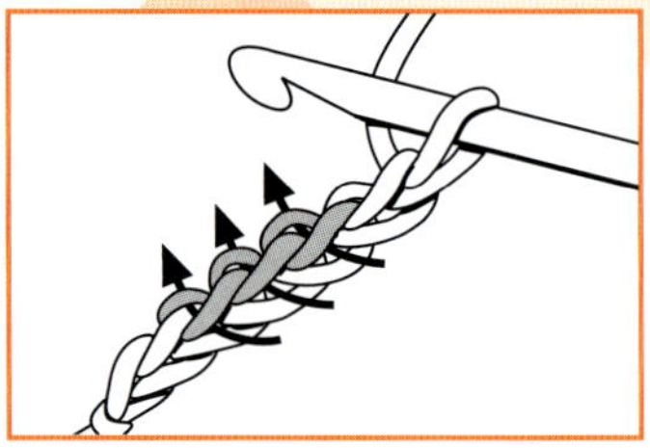

Fig. 5c

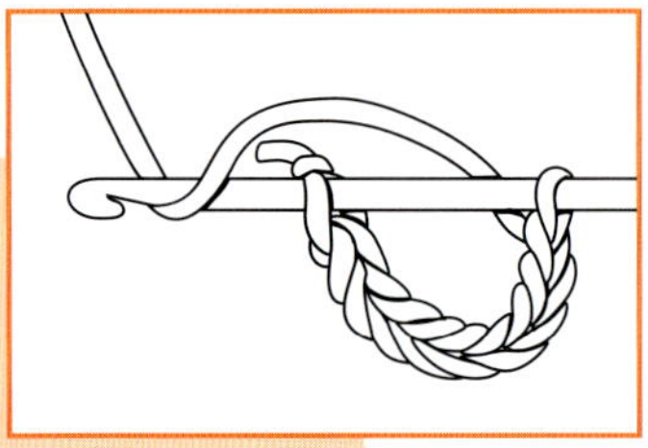

SLIP STITCH

To work a slip stitch, insert hook in stitch or space indicated, YO and draw through st and through loop on hook ***(Fig. 6)*** **(slip stitch made, *abbreviated slip st*)**.

Fig. 6

SINGLE CROCHET

Insert hook in stitch or space indicated, YO and pull up a loop, YO and draw through both loops on hook ***(Fig. 7)*** **(single crochet made, *abbreviated sc*)**.

Fig. 7

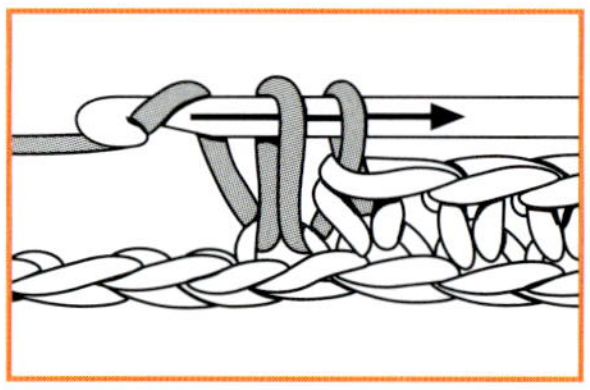

DOUBLE CROCHET

YO, insert hook in stitch or space indicated, YO and pull up a loop (3 loops on hook), YO and draw through 2 loops on hook ***(Fig. 8a)***, YO and draw through remaining 2 loops on hook ***(Fig. 8b)*** **(double crochet made, *abbreviated dc*)**.

Fig. 8a

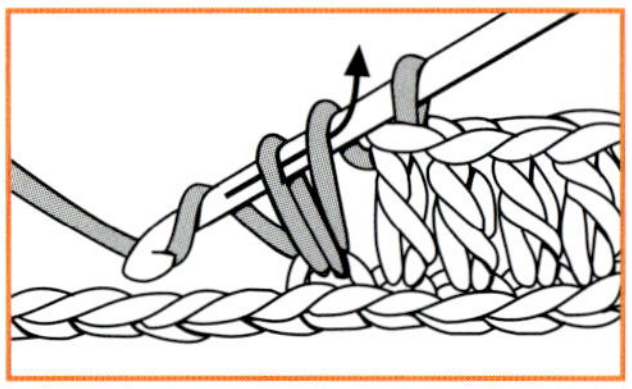

Fig. 8b